Tiptoe Into SCARY PLACES

ALIEN LANDING SITES

by Jessica Rudolph

Consultant: Ursula Bielski
Author and Paranormal Researcher
Founder of Chicago Hauntings, Inc.

BEARPORT

Credits

Cover, © VanderWolf Images/Fotolia, © kaisorn/Fotolia, and © nienora/Shutterstock; TOC, © SSSCCC/iStock; 4–5, © Anastasiia Malinich/Shutterstock, © Fer Gregory/Shutterstock, © xpixel/Shutterstock, and © motestockphoto/Shutterstock; 6, © MWaits/Shutterstock; 7T, © Chronicle/Alamy Stock Photo; 7B, © mdesigner125/Shutterstock; 8L, © Alexey Stiop/Alamy Stock Photo; 8R, © Zack Frank/Shutterstock; 9, © CrackerClips Stock Media/Shutterstock; 10, © The Charleston Gazette-Mail; 10–11, © Mary Terriberry/Shutterstock and © Triff/Shutterstock; 12, © The Charleston Gazette-Mail; 13L, Courtesy of the Braxton County Convention and Visitor's Bureau; 13R, © Eric Isselee/Shutterstock; 14, © Erik Lam/Shutterstock; 15, © Glenn Innes; 16, © UFO Casebook; 17, © UFO Casebook; 18, © Zastolskiy Victor/Shutterstock; 19, © Chris Mackler/Alamy Stock Photo; 20, © Fer Gregory/Shutterstock; 21, © bertos/iStock; 23, © adike/Shutterstock; 24, © EFKS/Shutterstock.

Publisher: Kenn Goin
Editor: J. Clark
Creative Director: Spencer Brinker
Photo Researcher: Thomas Persano
Cover: Kim Jones

Library of Congress Cataloging-in-Publication Data in process at time of publication (2018)
Library of Congress Control Number: 2017012326
ISBN-13: 978-1-68402-268-7 (library binding)

For more information, write to Bearport Publishing Company, Inc., 45 West 21st Street, Suite 3B, New York, New York 10010. Printed in the United States of America.

10 9 8 7 6 5 4 3 2 1

CONTENTS

ALIEN LANDING SITES

Boom! You hear an earsplitting noise behind your house, and you enter the dark woods to search for answers. What you find amazes you. A gigantic glowing green disc has crash landed! Through the clearing smoke, you see a door on the ship slowly open. You start to tremble. Who—or what—will appear?

Get ready to read four
spooky stories about **alien**
landing sites. Turn the page . . .
if you have the nerve!

5

World-Famous Aliens

Roswell, New Mexico

On June 13, 1947, a rancher in New Mexico heard a loud explosion during a storm. The next day, he discovered a long **trench** and odd **metallic** objects. His findings were reported to a nearby army base. Soon after, army officials removed the **wreckage.**

UFO CRASH SITE

UFO Museum - 114 N. Main - Roswell

6

Then the officials made a startling announcement: the remains were from a flying disc!

Objects from the wreckage

However, the army officials changed their story the next day. They now said the remains were from a **weather balloon.**

Soon rumors spread that the U.S. government was hiding **evidence** of an alien spaceship that had crash landed near Roswell. Some even said officials secretly removed alien bodies from the wreckage! Since then, the tiny town has become world-famous.

Visitors to Roswell can go to a **UFO** museum and see streetlamps that look like alien heads!

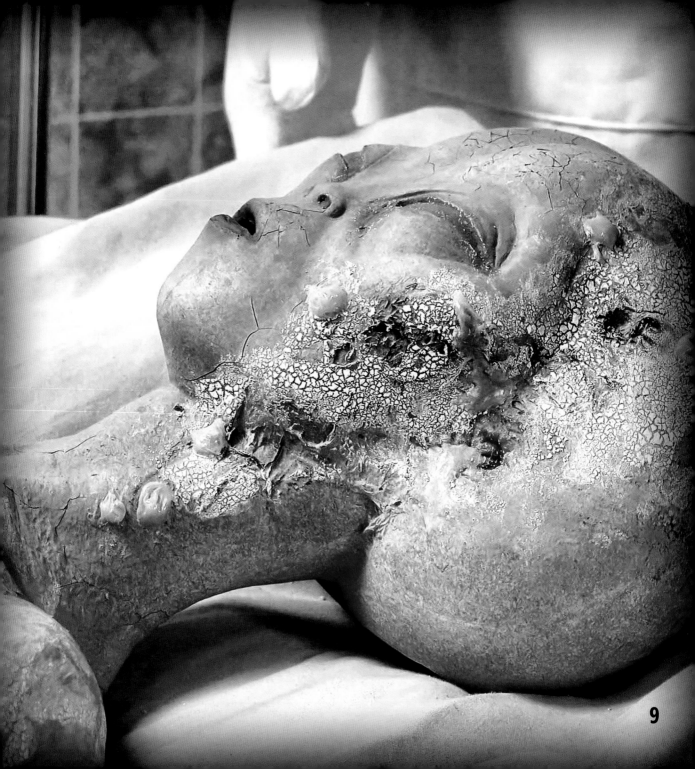

9

THE FLATWOODS MONSTER

Flatwoods, West Virginia

On the night of September 12, 1952, a group of boys saw a fiery light streak across the sky. They quickly ran to tell the mother of two of the boys.

The group of boys and the parent, Kathleen May, grabbed flashlights and hiked through the thick forest to **investigate.** Suddenly, a sickening mist burned their eyes and noses. Then they saw something terrifying.

An alien nearly 10 feet (3 m) tall was standing in the woods! The giant creature had claw-like hands and glowing eyes. It hissed and glided toward Kathleen and the boys. Then the alien took off in another direction.

The frightened group ran back to town to tell their story. The creature soon became known as the Flatwoods Monster.

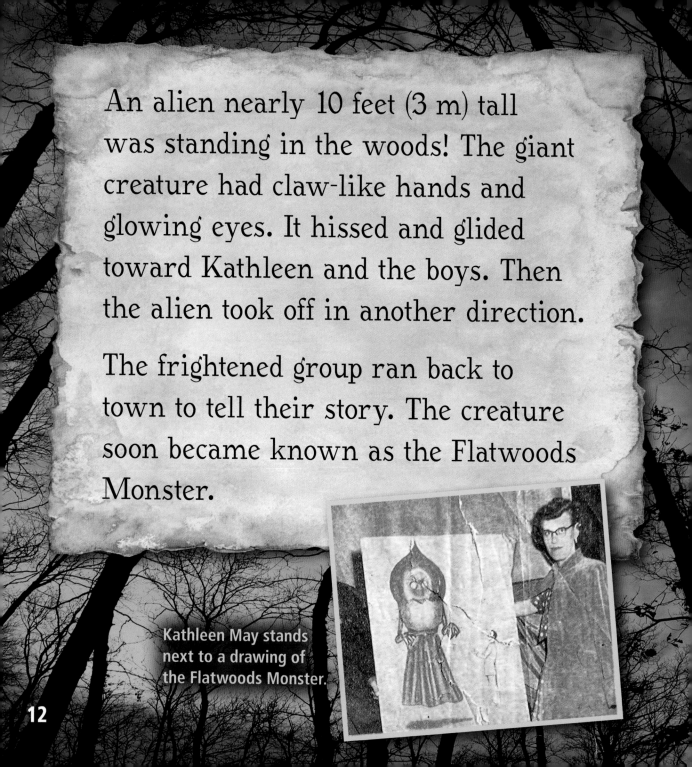

Kathleen May stands next to a drawing of the Flatwoods Monster.

Investigators said the fiery light and burning mist were probably caused by the crash of a **meteorite**. The "alien" may have been a barn owl in a tree.

13

ALMOST ABDUCTED

Livingston, Scotland

One day in November 1979, Robert Taylor came home with torn pants and cuts on his face. He told his wife and the police an amazing story. Aliens, he claimed, had tried to **abduct** him!

Robert had been walking his Irish setter in the damp woods when he came across a gray UFO **hovering** above the ground. He stood frozen in fear.

The Dechmont Woods
in Livingston, Scotland

15

Suddenly, two **spheres** covered with long spikes came out of the craft. Robert was shocked when the spikes hooked onto his pants and dragged him toward the craft. Then Robert blacked out. When he awoke, the UFO was gone.

Police went to the scene and found holes in the ground that looked like they'd been made by long spikes. Was Robert almost abducted by aliens?

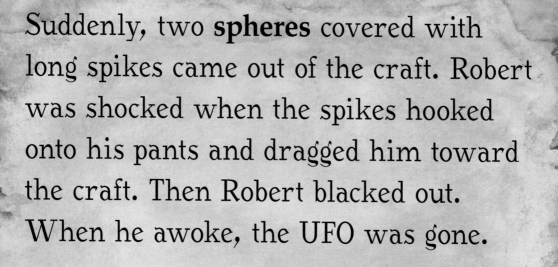

Robert Taylor at the site of his encounter

A drawing of the spacecraft and one of the spheres

Robert said the UFO was about 20 feet (6 m) wide.

Sworn to Secrecy?

Cape Girardeau, Missouri

One spring night in 1941, police asked Reverend William Huffman to pray at a site where an airplane had just crashed. The minister drove deep into the forest and met up with police, firefighters, and other government agents.

What he saw shocked him. The craft that had gone down was not a plane. And the victims were not human!

Cape Girardeau

Reverend Huffman saw a disc-shaped aircraft. There were three small, hairless creatures that had died in the crash—aliens! It's said that the strange beings had large heads and eyes and small mouths.

Huffman swore he would never tell anyone what he saw. However, when he went home, he told his family. After that, the story of what happened that night spread.

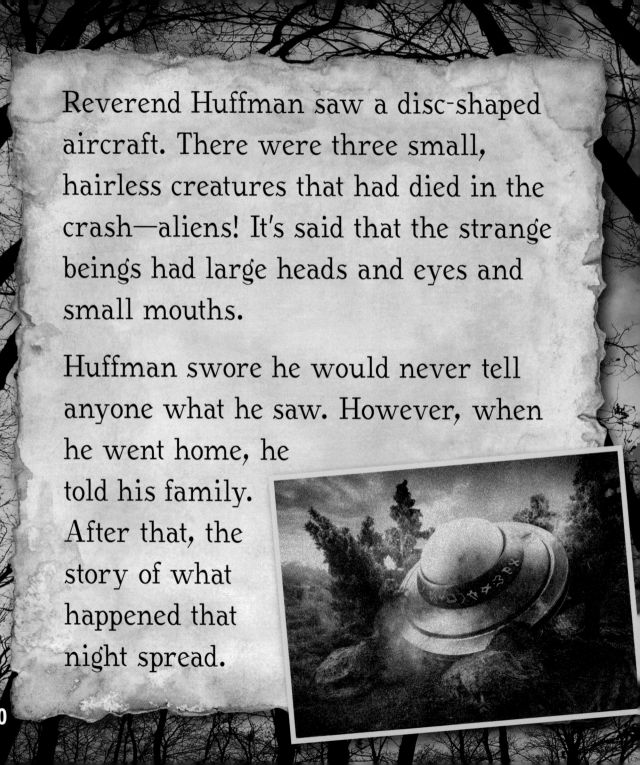

Many people who have reported seeing aliens have described them in a similar way—hairless with large heads and eyes and small mouths.

ALIEN LANDING SITES
AROUND THE WORLD

ROSWELL
New Mexico

Visit the most famous alien crash-landing site in the world.

CAPE GIRARDEAU
Missouri

A minister saw three aliens at this site—and couldn't keep it a secret!

FLATWOODS
West Virginia

Check out the scene where an alien monster with glowing eyes was once spotted.

LIVINGSTON
Scotland

Was a man almost abducted by beings from another planet in these Scottish woods?

Arctic Ocean

NORTH AMERICA

EUROPE

ASIA

Atlantic Ocean

Pacific Ocean

AFRICA

Pacific Ocean

SOUTH AMERICA

Indian Ocean

Atlantic Ocean

AUSTRALIA

Southern Ocean

ANTARCTICA

Glossary

abduct (ab-DUKT) to take someone away against his or her will

alien (AY-lee-uhn) a living being from another planet

evidence (EV-uh-duhnss) information and facts that help give proof of something

hovering (HUHV-ur-ing) flying in place without moving up, down, or side to side

investigate (in-VESS-tuh-gayt) to search for information to find out about something

metallic (meh-TAL-ik) containing or made of metal

meteorite (MEE-tee-ur-*ite*) a rock from space that has fallen to the ground

spheres (SFEERZ) ball-shaped objects

trench (TRENCH) a long, narrow hole

UFO (YOO EF OH) stands for Unidentified Flying Object; an object in the air that cannot be explained by human activities or nature

weather balloon (WETH-ur buh-LOON) a large balloon that carries instruments; it sends information about temperature, wind speed, and other weather conditions back to Earth

wreckage (REK-ihdj) pieces that remain after something has been badly damaged

Index

Read More

Halls, Kelly Milner. *Alien Investigation: Searching for the Truth About UFOs and Aliens.* Minneapolis, MN: Millbrook Press (2012).

Higgins, Nadia. *UFOs (Epic: Unexplained Mysteries).* Minneapolis, MN: Bellwether (2014).

Learn More Online

To learn more about alien landing sites, visit:
www.bearportpublishing.com/Tiptoe

About the Author

Jessica Rudolph lives in Connecticut. She has edited and written many books about history, science, and nature for children.